THE RULE

Conservative Political Centre

THE AUTHOR

SIR PATRICK MAYHEW, QC, MP was appointed Solicitor General in June 1983. He was previously Minister of State at the Home Office and Parliamentary Under-Secretary of State for Employment.

Sir Patrick has represented Tunbridge Wells in the House of Commons since February 1974.

He was called to the Bar by the Middle Temple in 1955, and became a Queen's Counsel in 1972.

This pamphlet is based on the lecture given by Sir Patrick Mayhew, QC, MP to the Conservative Political Centre meeting held in The Dome at Brighton on 10 October 1984.

CPC No. 0510/732

ISBN 0 85070 725 0

Published by the Conservative Political Centre
32 Smith Square, London SW1P 3HH and printed by
Strange the Printer, Streatfield Road, Heathfield, East Sussex TN21 8HX.

First published October 1984

THE RULE OF LAW

I AM MUCH FLATTERED by the unexpected compliment paid to me by David Knapp in the invitation to give this CPC Lecture.

The choice of subject he left to me. Plainly it ought to be some political or constitutional issue that is both topical and important. I decided that I should discuss the rule of law. None can doubt its importance, for it is the foundation of all our freedoms. As for its topicality, that has been only too readily apparent in 1984, which has seen the rule of law brought under such dangerous and sustained attack.

Let it never be forgotten, or concealed, that when (for example) someone organises the detonation of a bomb in Northern Ireland, or a mass attack upon police officers in Great Britain, and does so to attain an objective he knows he cannot attain without force, the principle is exactly the same in each case. Whether a bomb or a mob is used, he is attempting to overthrow the rule of law and establish the rule of force. If he were ever permitted to succeed, if through weariness, misguidedness or cowardice, a Government (if that would in the circumstances be the right noun) ever yielded to such tactics, the wall of the citadel would be breached, and that breach would grow wider and wider until all defence of democratic freedom ultimately ceased.

In a year when our TV screens have shown so frequently scenes in which the police are attacked by mobs determined to stop people exercising their lawful right to go into their place of work, it is easy to think of the rule of law only in the context of public order. After all, to most people the rule of law signifies the confidence that they will be safe within their own homes, and when going about their lawful business; that they won't be obstructed, assaulted or robbed in the street, pushed off a bus, or subjected to any other violence or intimidation. Freedom from these things is therefore of immense importance, and the defeat of those who seek to perpetrate them must be one of the highest obligations of Government.

But in this free country we depend on the rule of law to secure far more for us even than that. You will remember the kind of regime that was characterised in George Orwell's *Animal Farm*. There was order at Animal Farm all right; it was imposed by the rulers – those who were 'more equal' than others. But they were arbitrary, despotic rulers. What they said went, and the rest of the animals had no enforceable rights whatsoever. That represented the antithesis of the rule of law, because those who ruled were not subject to law themselves. It represented the rule of force.

It is sad that since *Animal Farm* was published we have in real life had so much experience of the techniques by which the rule of force is imposed. Initially, the rank and file are induced to be trusting. They comply readily and dutifully with what is asked of them, even though it calls for increasing sacrifices (as it always does). By the time they begin to see through the hypocrisy that has cloaked the true objective, which is the securing and entrenching of power for their leaders, it is too late and they are impotent. They must either join in, and collaborate with the rulers, as the leaders have now become, or become their victims.

In the United Kingdom, however, we have long insisted that we shall be protected by the rule of law. Therefore those who comprise the Government of the day are themselves subjected to the law. This has many wholesome consequences. No government, as we all know, may rule without answering to the electorate when five years are up. No-one may exercise force upon someone else without being answerable to the law. That is as true of a police officer as of anyone else, for ours is a citizen police force. We endow the police with no special privileges. Only their duties are special to them – and recent times have made vividly clear how arduous and dangerous these often are.

No politician in the United Kingdom may control the operational deployment of the police, nor turn the police into his own instrument.

No prosecution may be undertaken by the Crown in the United Kingdom for a politically partisan purpose. The supreme prosecuting authority in England and Wales is the Attorney General: in Scotland it is the Lord Advocate. Constitutionally each exercises these responsibilities judicially, taking into account the public interest. They are not here answerable to the Prime Minister, nor to the Cabinet: only to Parliament. In this respect they are unique among their colleagues, and this itself is a measure of our determination that our system of justice shall not be politicised.

Lastly, in the United Kingdom, underpinning and sustaining the entire complex, interlocking and sophisticated structure, is a Judiciary that is wholly independent and impartial.

We should avoid that complacency about our constitution which so strongly characterised our predecessors in the eighteenth century. We can, however, justly claim that our constitutional arrangements have up till now secured protection for the individual against oppression to a degree at least as effective as that enjoyed by any other people, and of course to a degree that would be regarded with incredulity by tens of millions in other countries if only they were permitted by their rulers to learn about them. Of course they will not be. Just consider, for example, the expectations with which Solidarity's leaders could appeal in Poland to a Judge appointed by a communist oligarchy and himself required to be a communist. They are unlikely to be sanguine.

It is, I believe, the effectiveness of our arrangements that calls forth the increasing scale of the attacks now being made on them. To the would-be autocrat it must be intolerable that the principle of the supremacy of the law should apply, as with us it does, to the Government itself, to every Minister comprising it; to every official serving it; to every trade union leader; to every employer, to every over-mighty subject, as well as to the humblest and least influential person in the land.

That it shall continue to apply and be accepted depends, I believe, first upon a Judiciary that is absolutely independent of Government, adjudicating without favour, affection or ill will. It also depends upon a police force of no less impartiality, whose powers are sensitively fashioned so as to impinge on the freedom of the individual only to the *minimum* extent that the public safety requires. And I believe that it depends, too, upon the content and administration of the law itself, which must not be seen to condone, or be impotent in the face of, conduct which to decent and sensible people is wrong and demanding of a remedy.

If the experience of the British people has given them confidence in these three pillars – an independent Judiciary, an impartial police force and law that is apt for the needs of justice – then they will wholeheartedly back, as they do at present, whatever necessary measures that are taken to uphold the rule of law against all the assaults of its enemies.

I am in no doubt that there are those who wish to overturn the whole constitutional structure that I have described. They are, however, astute enough in the main to realise that the British people are averse to political Big Bangs. They recognise equally that we are often unobservant, or at least unwary, of the process of progressive erosion. They know they can depend upon what has recently been called our genial tolerance, or laziness. Accordingly their tactic is to single out for repeated attack an individual pillar of the structure: it may be the Judiciary, the police, or the law itself. They seek to undermine and destroy the public confidence which is essential to the stability of each of these, a confidence which is still so strongly inherent in this country. They know it is highly probable that some prominent but naive people, who do not recognise the strategy underlying it and who would not endorse it if they did, will fall in with any campaign as it develops.

Whatever the motive, however, it is what is said and what is done that counts. I do not have primarily in mind isolated though notorious occasions from the past, like Mr Michael Foot's assault on the Industrial Relations Court with his reported contribution at the Scottish Miners' Gala in 1972: 'How long will it be before the cry goes up, let's kill all the judges?'. Perhaps that should be charitably ascribed to the hyperbole of a politician on an outing, a politician more nostalgic for the simplicities of the Peasants' Revolt than equipped for the industrial complexities of the late twentieth century.

Much more significant, as well as more recent, was Mr Dennis Skinner's accusation in the House of Commons, on 17th July this year, that the stakes in the GCHQ case were so high for the Prime Minister that she was quite capable of bribing the Appeal Court judges. On the Speaker 'naming' him, no fewer than 84 Labour Members voted in favour of Mr Skinner and against his withdrawal, including the Chairman of the Labour Party as well as one of its leading front bench spokesmen who is also a Privy Councillor.

Again, on 31st July Mr Martin Flannery was 'named' by the Speaker for referring to 'tame Tory judges'. The House of Commons then witnessed the Chairman of the Labour Party upbraiding Mr Kinnock for merely abstaining instead of voting for Mr Flannery.

Who can sensibly doubt that the Leninist Left, now so strongly dominant in the Labour Party, has created in that Party for the first time a real threat to the independence of the Judges? That is a measure, though not the only one, of the dissolute decline of the Labour Party. But much more important, it is a measure of the threat to the rule of law.

The Judges, of course, suffer the handicap of not being able to answer back when under such attack. Politicians hesitate to come to their defence, lest by doing so they involuntarily should seem to align the Judges with a political party. There is thus a real danger that by dint of repetition this kind of attack may indeed undermine the confidence of the public, and the confidence of the Judges themselves. If the latter were to occur, the consequences for judicial recruitment and quality are obvious. It needs therefore to be firmly stated what the true function of the Judges is, which is what I now propose to do.

If it is in the law that our rights and liberties are enshrined, it is in the Judges that the means lie whereby these are preserved and enforced. I will cite Lord Denning. The courts, he has said, 'stand between the Executive and the subject, alert to see that any coercive action is justified in law, and alert to see that a discretionary power is not exceeded or misused'.

In this country there is no one apart from the Judges upon whom the citizen can rely for impartial protection from misused Executive power. A member of Parliament may offer resistance to it, but he cannot invalidate it. The Ombudsmen for national and for local government may scrutinise and report, and they do so with great wisdom, but they cannot *require* a remedy. Yet so great is the scale on which the modern state intrudes into private life that the right of recourse to this jurisdiction of the Judges is precious indeed. It is a jurisdiction, it should be said, which they have had to develop for themselves. Successive Parliaments have in modern times declined to provide for this country any legislative statement determining the fundamental rights of the citizen in relation to the Executive.

It is true, I know, that the courts were rather late in adapting to the huge extension of State intervention. They tended to stand back, without examination, from any exercise by a Minister of a discretionary power. A Ministerial 'touch me not' was enough. But that is now long past; and recently Lord Diplock, thirty years a Judge and one who has had more to do with it than most, was able to say that the creation of a system of administrative justice was the greatest achievement of the law in his judicial lifetime.

Let us see how this has worked in practice. Do you recall the case of the TV licence fees? Mr Roy Jenkins was Home Secretary. He decided to put up the fee from 1st April 1975. The Home Office announced the new rate in plenty of time. But that gave to many people who already held a licence what Lord Denning described in the Court of Appeal as a bright idea. They renewed their licences just before 1st April, and of course at the old rate. There was a few days' overlap, but they would thereby avoid paying the new fee for almost a full year. They doubtless felt rather pleased with themselves.

The Home Office, however, was not pleased. The Minister already had power to revoke licences as well as to grant them, and he threatened this in the case of a number of people who refused to pay the higher fee. A certain Mr Congreve, however, took the Home Secretary to court. He challenged the legality of the revocation: and he won. The Court of Appeal said it was the Minister, or his Department, who had done wrong, not Mr Congreve. It was, said Lord Denning, a misuse of power.

All right, you may think the dispute a trivial one in those particular circumstances: but consider the principle which that case demonstrates. Things done by Ministers in the exercise of their discretion will be scrutinised and checked by the courts. The Judges won't substitute their own discretion for the Ministers': that is not their job. Their sole concern is to see that whatever discretionary power Parliament has given a Minister is exercised only for the purpose for which it is given, and on the basis of considerations relevant and not irrelevant to that purpose. That is a real safeguard against a malicious or merely capricious use of power. No one but the Judges can provide it.

Then you will remember, perhaps, the Tameside education case in 1976. The Secretary of State was told he had gone wrong in law in forbidding the newly elected Council to reverse their predecessors' policy of abolishing grammar schools on the ground that the available time was insufficient and that it would cause too much disruption.

The citizens in each case, faced with the official decision, would simply have had to lump it had it not been for the jurisdiction of the Judges.

I do not want to be thought unfairly selective in my examples. I cite as well, therefore, three cases where a court has of course not shrunk from holding our side to have gone wrong. We recall the famous case of Crichel Down, now many years ago, when the Ministry of Agriculture refused for improper reason to re-sell land to the original owner from whom it had earlier been compulsorily purchased. Much more recently Mr Justice Wolf, in July this year, held against the DHSS. He rejected the argument that the expense and labour of searching through millions of their records in order to identify a fairly small number of people who had admittedly been underpaid small amounts of benefit would be disproportionate in all the circumstances. The court held that it had to be done.

And then of course, Mr Justice Glidewell, trying the application at first instance, held against the Minister for the Civil Service on one aspect of the GCHQ case, which has yet to be finally determined by the House of Lords. I therefore say absolutely nothing about its merits. It is important to note, however, the Prime Minister's immediate response in the House of Commons to that original adverse judgment. She said,

> '. . . I, rightly, cannot overturn the decision of a court, and I would not wish to do so. I believe that people should be subject to a court of law. I also believe that, being subject to a court of law, they are entitled to use their right to go to appeal, especially on a very important matter such as this, which involves national security. I wish to make it clear that at the end of the judicial process Governments, of course, accept the courts' final ruling. *That is what the rule of law is all about.*'

I think we can discern from that Parliamentary Answer an eloquent contrast between the approach to the independence of the Judges, and to the rule of law, of the Prime Minister on the one hand and some of her opponents on the other.

From these examples, taken from many, of judicial decisions in favour of the citizen, each no doubt irritating to the Executive of the day, we can see at work that system of administrative justice to which Lord Diplock referred. Yet the achievement represented by its creation is an achievement of the Judges, not of Parliament. Discerning the need for it, the Judges have themselves developed an effective remedy through the concept of judicial review of discretionary action. Thus it may be seen that in the business of creating a jurisdiction under which the citizen may seek redress for the actions of the Executive, it is in truth the Judges who have made the running and not the Legislature elected to represent the citizens. I dare say that the Legislature's refusal over the years to act is not wholly unconnected with the perception that although a Party may be in opposition now it may itself form the government later, when judicial review of *its* actions could well prove inconvenient.

Lord Hailsham has already warned in this context of the dangers of an 'elective dictatorship'. There is of course a danger that if we continue to rely upon the Judges alone to ensure that justice is done between the citizen and the state, they will increasingly attract criticism that is political in nature. Political controversy is bad for Judges and bad for justice. They may have caught a measure of such criticism from different quarters in some of the cases I have mentioned. This, among other factors, leads many very distinguished people to argue for a Bill of Rights, a set of commonly agreed fundamental values which would, to some extent at least, be beyond political controversy and be incorporated into our law. It is one of the most complex issues of our time; but the difficulty I have with that proposal is that, to be effective, it would have to be much more, rather than less, likely to bring the Judges into the political arena.

I come now to the second constitutional pillar, the police. What should be their status and their powers? We are not a police state. We have never been a police state. We must never become a police state. I use that term in the accurate sense, the sense employed by Sir Winston Churchill in his classic Iron Curtain speech at Fulton, Missouri in 1946:

> 'In these states,' he said, 'control is enforced upon the common people by various kinds of all-embracing police Governments. The power of the state is exercised without restraint, either by dictators or by compact oligarchies operating through a privileged party and a political police.'

Anyone who knows the British police knows that they abhor being brought into the arena of political controversy. They have the best of reasons. Their authority stems from holding the ancient office of constable: they are not the servants of the Government of the day. It is this that wins for them the consent of the law-abiding community without which they could never discharge their duty of keeping the Queen's Peace and enforcing the criminal law.

In this country we have accordingly gone to great lengths to ensure that we do not, and cannot, have a political police. Chief constables have operational autonomy. Local police committees, part councillors and part magistrates, exercise only *non-operational* authority, and may not stray beyond this: theirs is the duty to secure the maintenance of an adequate and sufficient police force for their area. The Home Secretary has only a general responsibility, outside London, for the efficient policing of England and Wales as a whole, and as the police authority for the Metropolis he is constitutionally required to act without political partisanship. Police officers are required by their disciplinary code to be wholly impartial.

Of course, if their reputation for impartiality, and for being a non-political police force, could only be undermined, those who wish to overturn our constitutional structures would make great strides. That is why the extreme Left in localities which they control have set up units whose evident purpose is to undermine public confidence in the police. Large sums of the ratepayers' money are expended with this amiable purpose. I hope the District Auditors are examining every penny's worth with a gimlet eye.

The same reason explains their strenuous efforts, with which we are familiar, to portray officers struggling to hold back thousands of men as aggressive storm troopers in the pay of the Government, and the initiators of violence. (Incidentally, let those people when assembled in such numbers no longer be referred to as pickets. They are nothing of the sort: they are at best demonstrators and at worst rioters.) Police officers seen by the public to be using force start at a disadvantage in this country. By giving a partial account of what has happened, when the truth is that force was the only means by which the lawful rights of ordinary citizens could be protected, much valuable harm can be caused to public confidence.

Therefore the police today are in more than one sense highly vulnerable. This makes two things all the more important: first, that their powers should be sufficient, but not more than sufficient, to allow them to enforce the law; and secondly, that their powers should not be in doubt.

Neither of these conditions existed when Lord Whitelaw became Home Secretary in 1979. But thereafter the Philips Royal Commission on Police Powers and Criminal Evidence reported. It had been set up by Mr Merlyn Rees. Our Police and Criminal Evidence Bill contains provisions which in their essence were recommended by that Commission. The Commission had found that, if the police were to protect the public against the modern criminal, the present legislative morass governing the powers of the police (some of the most important of which have only local application) had to be reformed.

A great deal of bosh has been talked in opposition to this Bill, though from many useful suggestions it has benefited. People who say it will create a police state should go and see one first, and watch out how they behave when they are there.

Much of the attack on the Bill has centred on the provisions allowing a constable to stop and search someone for an offensive weapon if on reasonable grounds he suspects one is being carried. Our law has had a definition of an offensive weapon for many years and has made it an offence to carry one in public.

It depends, I suppose, on what you think is more important; the irritation and inconvenience of a search (of your top clothes only) or the ability of the police to prevent criminally disposed persons from hurting people.

I would only say that the Scottish police have had this power since 1981, and that almost one third of the people they stop on suspicion are found indeed to be carrying such a weapon.

Is it not better that before a knife, illegally carried, is thrust between someone's ribs at a football match, or a razor is brandished in the face of a baby whose mother is robbed in the street, it should have been first discovered and removed? That is why there ought to be a power to stop and search.

Of course there must be safeguards against abuse, and the Bill provides them. The officer may only act on reasonable suspicion, and he is answerable for his actions. Before any search takes place the officer must say who he is, what he is looking for and on what grounds his suspicion was aroused. He must generally make a record of what takes place, and he must inform the person that he can get a copy at any time up to a year later.

I do not believe that either the rule of law or respect for the law is enhanced by denying the people of England and Wales the protection that this power already so valuably confers in Scotland.

The other major attack on the Bill has suggested that for the first time it will permit detention of a suspect in a Police Station before a charge is made. This is not the case. Such detention is lawful at present. It takes place every day. But no time limit is placed on it: the maximum length of lawful detention is uncertain. It is subject to no judicial control, save by the insufficiently effective process of *habeas corpus*. It is a power whose limits are in doubt, and it is much too important and necessary a power for that to be allowed to continue.

What the Bill does do for the first time is to put a maximum time limit on such detention (96 hours), to limit any detention beyond 24 hours to serious arrestable offences, to require that it shall be authorised by a full Magistrates Court if it is to exceed 36 hours and by a further such hearing if it is sought to extend it beyond 72 hours. The suspect will have the right to legal aid at each of these judicial hearings.

How nice it would be if all the police had to investigate these days was the scrumping of apples, and the moonlit activities of the occasional Lincolnshire poacher. Unhappily we know that much graver crimes are committed by much more sophisticated people backed by much more powerful resources, to the great danger of the public. The public look to us to see that the law is sufficient to protect them.

This Government's reading of the public will is that, with proper safeguards for liberty, the police should not be denied the powers that they need to meet this modern challenge.

Edmund Burke, to whom one can so often turn with profit, has encapsulated the principle that we must apply:

> 'All Government,' he said, 'indeed every human benefit and enjoyment; every virtue, and every prudent act, is founded on compromise and barter. We balance inconveniences; we give and take; we remit some rights, that we may enjoy others . . . .'

This is a concept quite unknown, in my experience, to many single-issue pressure groups, but it is deeply rooted in the British character and its application is crucial to the ability of their police to enable them to live in freedom under the law.

I ask you to consider, lastly, the now familiar tactic of impugning the very validity of the law itself.

If on any basis at all it were to become accepted that we can pick and choose between laws which we will obey and laws which we will not, it would be laughable to speak of the rule of law and laughable to speak of order. Nothing must ever be done to give even spurious respectability to such a doctrine. Yet someone once said that the English are impossible to govern, except by themselves. That is merely to say that the English can only be ruled by consent. I am sure it is true, and moreover that it ought to be true.

> 'Nations,' wrote Burke, 'are not primarily ruled by laws; less by violence. Whatever original energy may be supposed

whether in force or regulation, the operation of both is, in truth, merely instrumental. Nations are governed by the same methods, and on the same principle, by which an individual without authority is often able to govern those who are his equals or his superiors: by a knowledge of their temper and a judicious management of it . . . *The temper of the people* amongst whom he presides ought therefore to be the first study of a statesman.'

The eighteenth century concept of the temper of the people remains, like eighteenth century architecture, both elegant and apt. What, then, is the temper of the British people? In some things it is uncomplicated. We hate bullying and oppression, and we believe that these should never be appeased or condoned. But in other respects I think it is more complex. I would suggest that the temper of the British people leads us, for example, to give our fiercest loyalty to what Burke called 'our little platoons'; to regard extreme opinions and extreme policies with scepticism, not to say distrust; to pay more heed to common sense and practical circumstances than to abstract political theory; to prefer to repair and restore rather than to demolish and start again; to demand that the Queen's Peace shall be preserved, and that none (including the Government, or any over-mighty subject) shall be above the law; but to require that *new* law shall be enforceable in practice as well as just in its conception.

It is, I think, beyond doubt that the Conservative Party led by Mrs Thatcher attracted such consent in the General Election of 1983 because it was seen, by reference to its record and its manifesto, to be far more in harmony with the temper of the people than was any of its opponents.

I am sure that pre-eminently we reflected the temper of the people in our legislation for the right to buy your council home; for ridding the taxpayer of the burdens of nationalisation; for stimulating independence, enterprise and competition; for the progressive dismantling of Labour's unfair and deeply debilitating trade union legislation, and for strengthening the arm of the courts in sentencing offenders.

The last two of these bear especially upon the rule of law, and topical events point to the importance of distinguishing very carefully between the civil and the criminal sanctions which they respectively provide.

Interference with other people's business by inducing people, whether employees, customers or suppliers, to break their contracts, has always been wrongful under English common law. But that wrong has always been a civil wrong, to be remedied by compensation, not a criminal wrong carrying the sanction of punishment. In other words, it has never been a crime. This means that the Crown cannot take the initiative in restraining such behaviour: that can only come from whoever is adversely affected.

But even before Mr Wilson's government, at the behest of the unions, so cynically curtailed people's rights to protection from interference with their businesses, and with their ability to keep their jobs, no such person was *compelled* to ask the courts for compensation or an injunction. He always had a right but never had a duty to do so. Now that we have restored those rights, and made them so much more effective, the same principle of course remains. If, for reasons that rightly or wrongly seem good to him, someone prefers *not* to seek a remedy in the courts, that is his choice, and so it should be.

I would only add that Mr Eddie Shah is one of those who have shown that if you *do* choose to use our employment legislation it comes fully up to specification. Mr Shah was held to be entitled to £125,000 damages, plus interest and costs and a permanent injunction, against the NGA for secondary action, and the Trade Union had to pay fines totalling £675,000 for contempt of court. The truth is that, to the chagrin of many of their officials, this legislation is very popular among trade unions members, of whom millions of course vote Conservative, because it enables their jobs to be protected once again from outside interference.

The nature and procedure of the criminal law is quite different. Here the Crown does take the initiative, though a private prosecutor can as well. For the punishment of offences committed in the course of public disorder there exists a very wide range of offences. As the Home Secretary explained in a speech this September, the most serious of them carry a maximum sentence of life imprisonment, and most people would say 'quite right too'. Many, I think, would add that they wish these cases could be brought on for trial more quickly. An independent prosecuting service responsible to the Attorney General, such as we propose, may well have an advantage here. The notion that 'Justice delayed is Justice denied' is as true today as in the days of Magna Carta; but some cases are very complex, and their preparation must not be made to suffer through undue haste.

When we came into office I believe the public thought there was almost as much wrong with the sentencing powers of the criminal courts as there was with the trade union legislation on the civil side. That was bad for the repute therefore for the public backing of the law. Lord Whitelaw's provisions in his Criminal Justice Act for widening the Courts' powers to deal with dangerous young offenders; for making parents liable to pay their children's fines; for making offenders compensate their victims; for community service orders, detention centres and for enabling prison sentences to be suspended only in part – these have all helped to remedy that, and the present Home Secretary is continuing this process.

Equally it must be acknowledged that if the public come to believe that sentences passed by the Judges are consistently too lenient, or alternatively too severe, that would be very dangerous. If they were thought to be too lenient, lynch law might result: if too severe, offences will not be reported. Either way the rule of law might suffer.

There is a temptation to overcome that danger by turning to mandatory sentences. It is one that must be firmly resisted. A Judge has to take into account not only the most lurid details – and it is so often only these that short newspaper reports can contain – but *all* the circumstances of the victim and those of the offender. Then, from the options made available by legislation, he must impose a sentence that meets the justice of the case. That is his responsibility alone, under our constitution, and therein perhaps both the highest art and the heaviest burden of judging lie.

Certainly it is right that sentencing principles should be laid down by the Lord Chief Justice and the Court of Appeal for the guidance of the Judges; and they are. It is also right, in my view, that the Court of Appeal should be given the opportunity to consider, at the request of the Attorney General, a particular case where there are good grounds for supposing too lenient a sentence has been passed. But the mandatory sentence forecloses on the judicial function. In practice it would have to be subject to the power of the Home Secretary, who is not a Judge, to intervene. It is not a device which should commend itself to a Party which has our concern for the individual.

I claim, therefore, that this legislation, so strongly in accord with the temper of the people, and perhaps as yet incomplete, has served to strengthen respect for the law itself.

One does not, however, have to look deeply into the electoral commitments of the Labour Party to find the promise of legislation which would be deeply damaging to the law. Every single item of Conservative trade union legislation would be repealed. Thus once again we should have immunity from all liability for secondary picketing and blacking, for action taken against employers with whom there is no dispute, and even to action taken only in support of some dispute occurring overseas. The funds of trade unions would once again be inviolate, and the closed shop would once more trample upon liberty with no liability for compensation. As for impartial justice, there is a dire warning to be found in the speech of Mr Paul Boateng,

Chairman of the GLC's police committee and a Parliamentary candidate at the general election, reported in the *Standard* on 18th September 1984. He said 'We must now make magistrates accountable to the party. That doesn't mean they will refer every decision to the party but the quality of their justice will be measured.' He added: 'They will have to accept the line on party justice.'

I come, therefore, to this conclusion. Democratic states submit to law so that there may be order without mere arbitrary government. If government is arbitrary the individual can have no enforceable rights. His very life is quite likely, in Hobbes' phrase, to be 'nasty, poor, mean, brutish and short'.

In this country we rightly, therefore, see it as the proper function of the law to be the provider, and the proper function of the Judges to be the protector, of the rights and liberties of the individual.

Alas, the influence and ideology of the extreme Left within the Party constituting the official Opposition now pose a real threat to the independence of the Judiciary. Secondly, they endanger the traditional separation of the police from the control of politicians. Thirdly, they represent by their extreme nature a threat to the respect in which the law as a whole is held. Because these are the three principal pillars supporting the rule of law, this too is endangered.

The British are, however, an experienced, sceptical and balanced people. We have seen many fanatics come, and sent them back from whence they came. We know that our liberties depend on the rule of law. If that is to be sustained, we know that it is necessary that 'we balance inconveniences; we give and take; we remit some rights, that we may enjoy others. . . .'

The British know, almost by instinct, that they must preserve upright and unshaken those constitutional pillars of which I have spoken.

The Conservative Party, therefore, must be seen to continue to uphold them faithfully. That should come easily to us, for we are after all the party of the Constitution. We must show the most resolute determination against those who would overthrow them, and who would impose the rule of force. Remembering that 'Nations are not ruled by laws alone' our first study must continue to be the 'temper of the people'. If, as I believe, we shall, we succeed in these tasks, then our Party may lay confident claim to the trust of the British people, and the future of our Nation will continue to unfold in freedom, under the rule of law.